WORKBOOK

INTERNAL FAMILY SYSTEMS

2023

Workbook by:
Therapy Courses

WELCOME

Welcome to the Internal Family Systems workbook. This workbook is intended to be worked through in order at first, but there are also references to points where you can go back and immerse yourself with the previous content.

There is a journal that accompanies this workbook that is specifically designed for the exercises in this book.

The exercises are mainly journalling based where you really look inside and try to understand your parts.

There are also mindfulness based exercises.

This workbook is not intended to replace therapy or your support systems. It is also not intended for anyone in crisis. If someone you know it is in crisis please contact your local mental health team or emergency services.

WHAT IS INTERNAL FAMILY SYSTEMS (IFS)?

Internal Family Systems is a type of psychotherapy developed by Richard Schwartz in the 1990s. IFS is based on the idea that everyone has multiple sub-personalities, or "parts," within themselves, and that these parts can be organized into a system. The goal of IFS is to help individuals become more aware of their internal systems and work towards developing a healthier and more harmonious relationship with their parts.

In IFS therapy, individuals are encouraged to identify and separate from their parts, in order to gain a better understanding of them. This involves creating a safe and supportive environment where individuals can explore their internal world without judgment or criticism.

IFS therapy also emphasizes the importance of cultivating Self-leadership, which involves accessing one's true Self - a core state of being that is characterized by compassion, curiosity, and confidence. By connecting with their Self, individuals can develop a greater sense of inner harmony and learn to manage their parts more effectively.

Overall, IFS is a holistic and integrative approach to therapy that seeks to help individuals heal and grow by exploring their internal world and developing a more compassionate and understanding relationship with themselves.

OVERVIEW OF THE "PARTS" THEORY

The concept of parts is central to the IFS model and refers to different aspects of an individual's personality, emotions, and behaviours.

According to IFS theory, each individual has a "Self" at the core of their being, which is characterized by qualities such as compassion, curiosity, and calmness. However, this Self can become obscured by various parts that can emerge as a result of life experiences, including trauma, neglect, and attachment issues. These parts can take on different roles, such as protectors, managers, or exiles, and may exhibit a range of emotions and behaviours.

Protector parts are often the first to emerge, and their primary role is to shield the Self from harm. These parts can be highly reactive and may exhibit behaviours such as anger, anxiety, or numbness. Examples of protector parts include the inner critic, the perfectionist, or the caretaker.

Manager parts, on the other hand, are more strategic in their approach and seek to manage or control the environment in order to protect the Self. These parts can be highly organized and goal-oriented and may exhibit behaviours such as overworking, overthinking, or compulsive behaviour. Examples of manager parts include the controller, the planner, or the intellectualizer.

Exile parts are often the most vulnerable parts of an individual's internal world and carry painful emotions or memories. These parts may have been suppressed or denied by protectors or managers and can contribute to feelings of shame, depression, or anxiety. Examples of exile parts include the wounded child, the traumatized part, or the abandoned part.

The goal of IFS therapy is to help individuals develop a deeper understanding and connection with all of their parts, including the Self. Through this process, individuals can learn to identify and regulate their emotions, heal past wounds, and cultivate a greater sense of inner peace and harmony. IFS therapists often use a range of techniques, such as guided visualization, mindfulness, and parts dialogue, to help individuals work with their parts and move towards greater self-awareness and healing.

THE SELF

The "Self" refers to the core of an individual's being - their natural, calm, and compassionate state of being. According to IFS, everyone has a Self, regardless of their life experiences or challenges. The Self is seen as a central and important aspect of IFS therapy, as it is believed to be the foundation of healing and transformation.

The Self is characterized by a number of different qualities, including calmness, clarity, curiosity, compassion, and connectedness. When an individual is in touch with their Self, they are able to access these qualities and respond to situations in a more adaptive and effective way.

In contrast, when an individual is not in touch with their Self, they may experience a range of symptoms, including anxiety, depression, and disconnection. This is often due to the presence of "parts" - different aspects of an individual's personality that have developed in response to past experiences and are designed to protect them from harm.

IFS therapy emphasizes the importance of helping individuals connect with their Self in order to heal and integrate their different parts. This involves cultivating a sense of curiosity and compassion towards their parts, and working towards identifying and addressing the underlying fears and needs of those parts.

By developing a deeper connection with their Self, individuals can begin to access the qualities of calmness, clarity, and compassion that are inherent within them. This can help them to better regulate their emotions, manage stress, and cultivate greater resilience in the face of life's challenges.

Overall, the Self is seen as a central and important aspect of IFS therapy, as it provides a foundation for healing, growth, and transformation. By cultivating a deeper understanding and connection with their Self, individuals can begin to access their innate capacity for healing and integration.

THE PROTECTOR

Protector parts often emerge in response to perceived threats, whether internal or external. They may be triggered by past traumas or current stressors, and can exhibit behaviours such as anxiety, anger, or numbness.

Protector parts can take on different forms and roles, such as the inner critic, the perfectionist, or the caretaker.

The inner critic is a common type of protector part that can be particularly harsh and critical towards the self. It may use negative self-talk and undermine the individual's self-esteem, often with the intention of protecting the self from failure or rejection.

The perfectionist is another type of protector part that can be highly critical and demanding of the self. It may have high standards and expectations, and may push the individual to strive for perfection in order to avoid feeling inadequate or vulnerable.

The caretaker is a protector part that may take on a nurturing and caretaking role towards others, often at the expense of the self. It may prioritize the needs of others over the individual's own needs, with the intention of maintaining relationships and avoiding conflict.

While protector parts may initially serve a useful function in protecting the individual from harm, they can also become problematic when they become too rigid or extreme.

EXILES

These exiled parts of the self are often associated with intense emotions, memories, or experiences that are too overwhelming to process at the time of the trauma.

Exiles may manifest in a variety of ways, including depression, anxiety, panic attacks, self-harm, substance abuse, or dissociation. They can also contribute to feelings of shame, guilt, or worthlessness, as the individual may believe that these parts of themselves are flawed or undesirable.

In IFS therapy, the goal is to help individuals develop a compassionate and curious relationship with their exiles, in order to facilitate healing and integration. This may involve identifying the specific exiled parts of the self, exploring the memories and emotions associated with these parts, and working to build trust and connection with them.

The IFS worksheets help the individual access their inner resources, such as self-compassion, self-soothing, and self-care, in order to support the healing process. By developing a stronger connection with their exiled parts and integrating them into their overall sense of self, individuals can experience greater wholeness, resilience, and well-being.

MANAGERS

Managers can be seen as protectors that are responsible for maintaining a sense of order, predictability, and safety in the individual's life.

Managers can manifest in a variety of ways, including perfectionism, workaholism, overachievement, controlling behaviours, and rigid thinking patterns. They may also contribute to feelings of anxiety or stress, as the individual may feel pressure to maintain their sense of control and avoid any situations that could activate their exiled parts.

The goal is to help individuals develop a compassionate and collaborative relationship with their managers, in order to reduce their need for control and promote greater flexibility and openness in their lives. This may involve identifying the specific managers that are active in the individual's life, exploring their beliefs and motivations, and working to understand how they may be contributing to feelings of stress or anxiety.

FIREFIGHTERS

Firefighters refer to the parts of the self that take action to protect the individual in response to the activation or expression of exiled parts. Firefighters can be seen as emergency responders that are responsible for containing and managing any situations that threaten the individual's sense of safety or well-being.

Firefighters can manifest in a variety of ways, including impulsive or destructive behaviours, substance abuse, dissociation, self-harm, or other extreme responses to stress or trauma. They may also contribute to feelings of shame or guilt, as the individual may feel out of control or disconnected from their actions during a firefighting episode.

The goal is to develop a compassionate and collaborative relationship with their firefighters, in order to reduce their need for emergency action and promote greater self-care and emotional regulation. This may involve identifying the specific firefighters that are active in the individual's life, exploring their beliefs and motivations, and working to understand how they may be contributing to feelings of stress or overwhelm.

EXERCISES

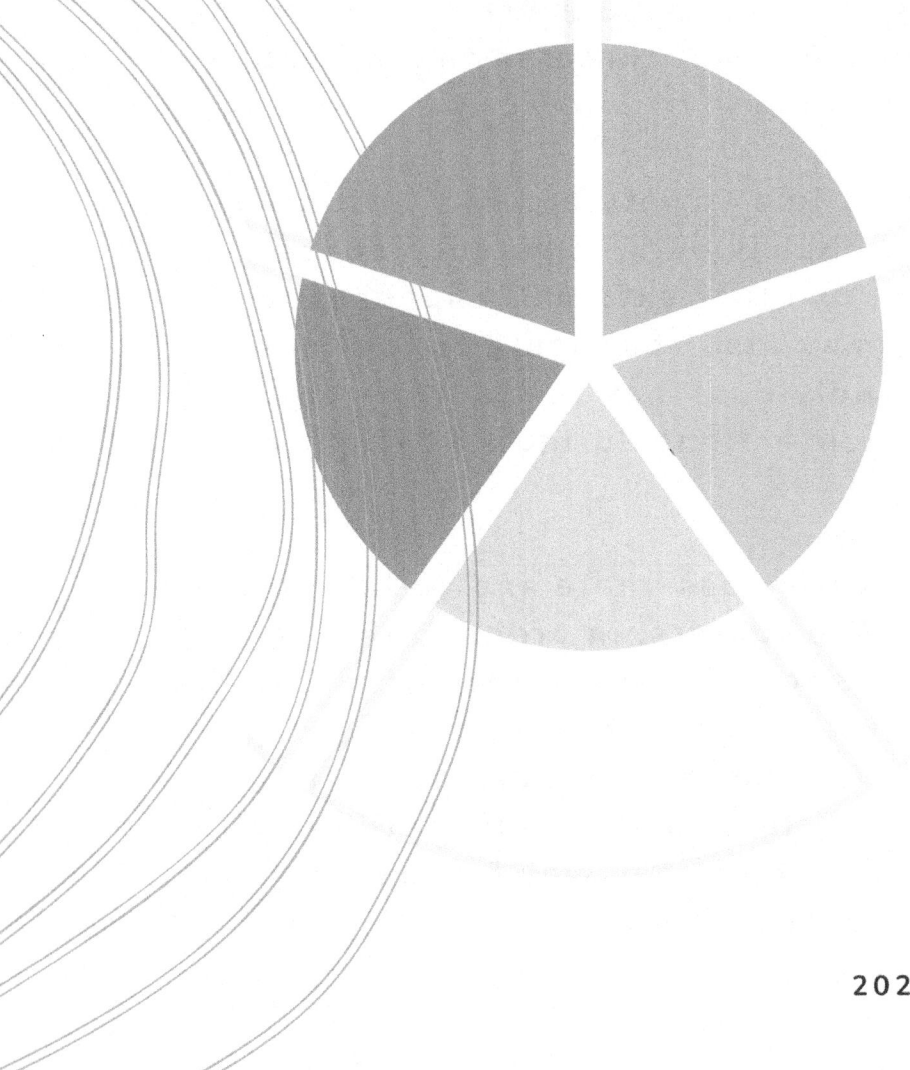

2023

Workbook by:
Therapy Courses

INTRO TO IFS

UNDERSTANDING THE BASICS OF IFS

Objective: Familiarize yourself with the key concepts of Internal Family Systems (IFS) therapy and recognize how they apply to your own internal world.

1. Begin by reading the following summary of the IFS model:

The Internal Family Systems model views the mind as a system of interacting parts, much like a family. Each part has its own purpose, feelings, and beliefs. IFS identifies three main types of parts:

- Managers: These parts are proactive and work to maintain control and stability in your life. They are responsible for planning, organizing, and protecting you from potential harm.
- Firefighters: These parts are reactive and respond to immediate threats or crises. They use impulsive behaviours, like numbing or distracting, to protect you from overwhelming emotions or memories.
- Exiles: These parts hold painful memories, emotions, or beliefs that have been "exiled" from conscious awareness. They may be vulnerable, sensitive, or carry unresolved trauma.

At the centre of this system is the True Self, which is your core essence. It is characterized by qualities like curiosity, compassion, confidence, and creativity. The goal of IFS therapy is to help you access and strengthen your True Self so that it can effectively lead and heal your parts.

2. Reflect on the following questions in a journal:

- Can you think of any situations in your life where Manager, Firefighter, or Exile parts have emerged? Provide examples for each type of part.

- How do you imagine your True Self? What qualities do you associate with it?

- Are there any aspects of the IFS model that resonate with you or feel particularly relevant to your life?

3. Once you have completed your reflection, take a few moments to think about how this new understanding of your internal system might influence your self-awareness and personal growth journey.

4. As you progress through the workbook, consider revisiting this exercise periodically to solidify your understanding of the IFS model and to reflect on any new insights or experiences.

THE TRUE SELF

IDENTIFYING YOUR TRUE SELF

Objective: Connect with and recognize the qualities of your True Self to enhance self-awareness and empower personal growth.

Instructions:

1. Find a quiet space where you can relax and focus without distractions. Take a few deep breaths and try to quiet your mind.

2. Once you feel centred, reflect on the following qualities that characterize the True Self:

- Compassion
- Curiosity
- Confidence
- Creativity
- Calmness
- Clarity
- Courage
- Connectedness

3. As you consider each quality, ask yourself the following questions and jot down your answers in your journal:

- Which of these qualities resonate most with me when I am at my best?

- Are there any specific moments or experiences in my life when I have felt connected to these qualities?
- How do I feel when I am connected to my True Self? What emotions or sensations arise?

4. After reflecting on your True Self, write a brief description of how you envision it. Include the qualities you identified as most resonant and any additional characteristics that feel relevant.

5. Consider creating a symbol, image, or phrase that represents your True Self. This can serve as a reminder or anchor when you want to connect with your True Self during challenging times or throughout your IFS journey.

6. As you progress through the workbook, use your True Self as a reference point to guide your self-exploration and growth. Regularly check in with your True Self to ensure that it is leading your internal system and cultivating a sense of balance and harmony.

THE TRUE SELF

STRENGTHING YOUR CONNECTION TRUE SELF

Objective: Connect with and recognize the qualities of your True Self to enhance self-awareness and empower personal growth.

Instructions:

1. Find a quiet space where you can relax and focus without distractions. Take a few deep breaths and try to quiet your mind.
2. Review the description, symbol, image, or phrase you created to represent your True Self in Exercise 2.
3. Choose one or more of the following practices to help you strengthen your connection with your True Self. Be open to experimenting with different approaches to discover what works best for you.

- Meditation: Set aside time each day to meditate and focus on your True Self qualities. This can help you develop a stronger connection with your core essence and increase your ability to access your True Self during daily life.

- Journaling: Regularly write about your experiences with your True Self, noting when you feel connected or disconnected from it. This practice can help you track your progress and identify patterns or triggers related to your connection.

- Mindfulness: Incorporate mindfulness practices, such as deep breathing or body scans, into your daily routine to help you stay present and connected with your True Self.
- Visualization: Use visualization techniques to imagine your True Self as a source of light, warmth, or energy within you. As you breathe, envision this energy expanding to fill your entire body and radiate outward, reinforcing your connection with your True Self.

3. Commit to engaging in your chosen practice(s) consistently for at least two weeks. Document your experiences in your journal, paying attention to any changes in your connection with your True Self.
4. After the two-week period, reflect on the following questions in your journal:

- Which practice(s) did I find most helpful in strengthening my connection with my True Self? Why?
- What changes, if any, have I noticed in my connection with my True Self? How has this affected my daily life or my work with my internal system?
- Are there any adjustments or additional practices I want to explore to further strengthen my connection with my True Self?

6. Continue to engage in these practices and adjust them as needed, ensuring that your True Self remains a guiding force in your personal growth journey.

THE MANAGER PARTS

IDENTIFYING YOUR MANAGER PARTS

Objective: Recognize and understand your Manager parts to gain insight into their roles and functions within your internal system.

Instructions:

1. Begin by familiarizing yourself with the role of Manager parts in the IFS model:

Manager parts are proactive and work to maintain control and stability in your life. They are responsible for planning, organizing, and protecting you from potential harm. Some common Manager parts include the Perfectionist, the Planner, the Critic, the Caretaker, and the Pleaser.

2. Reflect on your own internal system and consider the following questions:

- Which Manager parts do I recognize within myself? Are there any that stand out as particularly dominant or influential?
- What specific roles or functions do these Manager parts serve in my life? How do they try to maintain control or protect me?

Example:

- The Perfectionist: Ensures that I always perform at my best and avoid mistakes or criticism.

3. Once you have identified your Manager parts, take a moment to consider the following questions:

- How do these Manager parts influence my thoughts, feelings, and actions?
- Are there any situations in which my Manager parts are particularly active or noticeable?

4. As you progress through the workbook, use this list of Manager parts as a reference for further exploration and self-discovery. You will have opportunities to deepen your understanding of these parts and learn strategies for working with them in a more balanced and harmonious way.

THE MANAGER PARTS

EXPLORING THE ROLES OF YOUR MANAGER PARTS

Objective: Gain deeper insight into the roles and functions of your Manager parts to better understand their motivations and influence within your internal system.

Instructions:

1. Review the list of Manager parts you created in Exercise 4. Choose one Manager part that you would like to explore further.

2. Reflect on the following questions, writing your answers in your journal:

- What specific situations or circumstances activate this Manager part?

- What are the underlying motivations or fears driving this Manager part's actions? How does it aim to protect or support me?

- Can I recall any specific experiences or memories when this Manager part played a significant role in my thoughts, feelings, or actions?

3. Now, imagine having a conversation with this Manager part. Write a dialogue between you (your True Self) and the Manager part, addressing the following topics:

- Express appreciation for the part's efforts to protect and support you.

- Ask the part to share its concerns or fears and its perspective on its role within your internal system.

- Offer reassurance that you (your True Self) are here to listen, understand, and collaborate with the part.

Example:

True Self: Thank you, Perfectionist, for always trying to help me perform at my best. I know you have good intentions. Can you tell me more about your concerns and why you feel the need to be so vigilant?

Perfectionist: I'm afraid that if you make mistakes or don't meet high standards, others will criticize or reject you. I want to keep you safe from that pain, so I push you to excel.

True Self: I appreciate your efforts to protect me, and I understand your concerns. I'm here to listen and work together with you to find a healthy balance.

4. After completing the dialogue, reflect on the following questions in your journal:

- What new insights or perspectives did I gain about this Manager part?

- Are there any patterns or beliefs that I need to address or reevaluate in relation to this Manager part?

5. Repeat this exercise for any additional Manager parts you wish to explore further. As you progress through the workbook, continue to engage in dialogues with your Manager parts and seek to understand their roles and motivations to foster a more balanced and harmonious internal system.

THE FIREFIGHTER PARTS

IDENTIFY YOUR FIREFIGHTER PARTS

Objective: Recognize and understand your Firefighter parts to gain insight into their roles and functions within your internal system.

Instructions:

1. Begin by familiarizing yourself with the role of Firefighter parts in the IFS model:

Firefighter parts are reactive and respond to immediate threats or crises. They use impulsive behaviours, such as numbing, distracting, or avoiding, to protect you from overwhelming emotions or memories. Some common Firefighter parts include the Procrastinator, the Overeater, the Workaholic, the Escapist, and the Worrier.

2. Reflect on your own internal system and consider the following questions:

- Which Firefighter parts do I recognize within myself? Are there any that stand out as particularly dominant or influential?

- What specific roles or functions do these Firefighter parts serve in my life? How do they try to protect me or cope with difficult emotions?

3. In your journal, create a list of your Firefighter parts. For each part, briefly describe its primary role or function.

Example:

- The Procrastinator: Helps me avoid feelings of anxiety or overwhelm by delaying tasks or decisions.

4. Once you have identified your Firefighter parts, take a moment to consider the following questions:

- How do these Firefighter parts influence my thoughts, feelings, and actions?
- Are there any situations in which my Firefighter parts are particularly active or noticeable?

5. As you progress through the workbook, use this list of Firefighter parts as a reference for further exploration and self-discovery. You will have opportunities to deepen your understanding of these parts and learn strategies for working with them in a more balanced and harmonious way.

THE FIREFIGHTER PARTS

UNDERSTANDING THE PURPOSE OF YOUR FIREFIGHTER PARTS

Objective: Gain deeper insight into the roles and functions of your Firefighter parts to better understand their motivations and influence within your internal system.

Instructions:

1. Review the list of Firefighter parts you created in Exercise 6. Choose one Firefighter part that you would like to explore further.
2. Reflect on the following questions, writing your answers in your journal:

- What specific situations or circumstances activate this Firefighter part?
- What are the underlying motivations or fears driving this Firefighter part's actions? How does it aim to protect or support me?
- Can I recall any specific experiences or memories when this Firefighter part played a significant role in my thoughts, feelings, or actions?

3.Now, imagine having a conversation with this Firefighter part. Write a dialogue between you (your True Self) and the Firefighter part, addressing the following topics:

- Express appreciation for the part's efforts to protect and support you.
- Ask the part to share its concerns or fears and its perspective on its role within your internal system.
- Offer reassurance that you (your True Self) are here to listen, understand, and collaborate with the part.

Example:

True Self: Thank you, Procrastinator, for trying to protect me from feelings of anxiety or overwhelm. I know you have good intentions. Can you tell me more about your concerns and why you feel the need to delay tasks or decisions?

Procrastinator: I'm afraid that you'll become too stressed or overwhelmed if you face everything head-on. I want to keep you safe from that pain, so I help you put things off until you feel more ready to handle them.

True Self: I appreciate your efforts to protect me, and I understand your concerns. I'm here to listen and work together with you to find a healthy balance.

4. After completing the dialogue, reflect on the following questions in your journal:

- What new insights or perspectives did I gain about this Firefighter part?
- Are there any patterns or beliefs that I need to address or reevaluate in relation to this Firefighter part?

5. Repeat this exercise for any additional Firefighter parts you wish to explore further. As you progress through the workbook, continue to engage in dialogues with your Firefighter parts and seek to understand their roles and motivations to foster a more balanced and harmonious internal system.

THE EXILED PARTS

IDENTIFYING YOUR EXILED PARTS

Objective: Recognize and understand your Exiled parts to gain insight into their roles and functions within your internal system.

1. Begin by familiarizing yourself with the role of Exiled parts in the IFS model:

Exiled parts hold painful memories, emotions, or beliefs that have been "exiled" from conscious awareness. They may be vulnerable, sensitive, or carry unresolved trauma. These parts are often hidden or protected by Manager and Firefighter parts.

2. Reflect on your own internal system and consider the following questions:

- Which Exiled parts do I recognize within myself? Are there any that stand out as particularly significant or influential?

- What specific emotions, memories, or beliefs do these Exiled parts hold? How have they been impacted by past experiences?

3. In your journal, create a list of your Exiled parts. For each part, briefly describe the emotions, memories, or beliefs it holds.

Example:

- The Abandoned Child: Holds feelings of loneliness and unworthiness stemming from childhood experiences of rejection or neglect.

4. Once you have identified your Exiled parts, take a moment to consider the following questions:

- How do these Exiled parts influence my thoughts, feelings, and actions?
- Are there any situations in which my Exiled parts are particularly active or noticeable?

5. As you progress through the workbook, use this list of Exiled parts as a reference for further exploration and self-discovery. You will have opportunities to deepen your understanding of these parts and learn strategies for working with them in a more compassionate and healing way.

THE EXILED PARTS

EXPLORING STORIES OF YOUR EXILED PARTS

1. Review the list of Exiled parts you created in Exercise 8. Choose one Exiled part that you would like to explore further.

2. Reflect on the following questions, writing your answers in your journal:

- What specific emotions, memories, or beliefs does this Exiled part hold? How have they been impacted by past experiences?

- Can I recall any specific experiences or memories that may have contributed to the formation of this Exiled part?

3. Now, imagine having a conversation with this Exiled part. Write a dialogue between you (your True Self) and the Exiled part, addressing the following topics:
- Express empathy and understanding for the part's pain or struggles.

- Ask the part to share its story and any emotions, memories, or beliefs it holds.

- Offer reassurance that you (your True Self) are here to listen, understand, and support the part's healing and integration.

Example:

True Self: I'm so sorry that you've been carrying the pain of abandonment and unworthiness, Abandoned Child. I want to understand your story and help you heal. Can you share more about your experiences and the emotions you hold?

Abandoned Child: I remember feeling lonely and unimportant when I was left alone or ignored as a child. It makes me believe that I'm not worthy of love or attention.

True Self: I hear your pain, and I want you to know that you are valuable and deserving of love. I'm here to support you and help you heal from these past experiences.

4. After completing the dialogue, reflect on the following questions in your journal:

- What new insights or perspectives did I gain about this Exiled part?

- Are there any patterns or beliefs that I need to address or reevaluate in relation to this Exiled part?

Repeat this exercise for any additional Exiled parts you wish to explore further. As you progress through the workbook, continue to engage in dialogues with your Exiled parts, seeking to understand their stories and offer compassionate support for their healing and integration within your internal system.

BUILDING SELF-AWARENESS

RECOGNIZING YOUR PARTS IN ACTION

Objective: Develop your ability to recognize when your parts are active and influencing your thoughts, feelings, and actions in daily life.

Instructions:

1. Review the lists of Manager, Firefighter, and Exiled parts you created in Exercises 4, 6, and 8.

2. Over the course of one week, commit to observing yourself in various situations and settings, paying close attention to your thoughts, feelings, and actions.

3. During this week, whenever you notice a part becoming active or influencing your behaviour, take a moment to acknowledge it. Record the following information in your journal:

- Which part was active? (Manager, Firefighter, or Exiled)

- What situation or circumstance triggered the part's activation?

- How did the part influence your thoughts, feelings, or actions?

Example:

- Active part: Procrastinator (Firefighter)
- Trigger: Facing a difficult task at work
- Influence: Delayed starting the task, felt anxious and overwhelmed

4. At the end of the week, review your journal entries and reflect on the following questions:

- Were there any patterns or recurring themes in the situations that triggered your parts?

- Were certain parts more active or influential than others? If so, why do you think that is?

- How did recognizing and acknowledging your parts in action impact your thoughts, feelings, or actions in those situations?

5. Use your observations and reflections to deepen your understanding of your internal system and its dynamics. Continue practising self-awareness to recognize when your parts are active, and consider how this knowledge can guide your personal growth and self-healing journey.

BUILDING SELF-AWARENESS
___

JOURNALING TO ENHANCE SELF-AWARENESS

Objective: Use journaling as a tool to increase self-awareness, explore your internal system, and promote self-discovery and personal growth.

Instructions:

1. Choose a quiet, comfortable space where you can write without distractions.

2. Set aside time each day or week for journaling, depending on your preferences and schedule. Consistency is key to reaping the benefits of this practice.

3. Use the following journal prompts as a starting point to explore your thoughts, feelings, experiences, and parts. Feel free to add your own prompts or adjust these to better suit your needs.

- What emotions did I experience today, and which parts were associated with those emotions?

- Describe a situation where a part was activated or influential. How did it impact my thoughts, feelings, or actions? How did I respond to this part?

- Reflect on a conversation or interaction I had with one of my parts. What insights did I gain from this dialogue?

- What challenges did I face today or this week? Which parts were involved, and how did they react or contribute to the situation?

- What successes or personal growth moments did I experience today or this week? How did my parts contribute to or respond to these accomplishments?

- Are there any unresolved emotions, memories, or beliefs that I need to explore or address with my parts? How can I approach this healing work with compassion and curiosity?

4. As you write, try to maintain a nonjudgmental and open-minded attitude. Allow yourself the freedom to express your thoughts and emotions authentically.

5. Periodically review your journal entries to identify patterns, recurring themes, or areas of growth. Reflect on any insights or discoveries you have made through journaling and consider how you can apply this knowledge to your ongoing personal development.

6. Continue to use journaling as a tool for self-awareness and self-discovery, adapting the practice to suit your evolving needs and preferences. Remember that the purpose of journaling is to better understand your internal system, foster self-compassion, and support your growth and healing journey.

CULTIVATING SELF-COMPASSION

DEVELOPING A COMPASSIONATE VOICE IN YOUR HEAD

Objective: Cultivate a compassionate inner voice to promote self-acceptance, self-kindness, and emotional healing within your internal system.

Instructions:

1. Reflect on your current inner dialogue. Consider the following questions:

- How do I speak to myself when I make a mistake, face a challenge, or experience a setback?
- Are there specific parts (e.g., Manager or Firefighter) that tend to be critical, harsh, or judgmental in their inner dialogue?

2. In your journal, write down some examples of negative or critical self-talk that you commonly experience.

Example:

- "I can't believe I messed up again. I'm such a failure."

Now, imagine a compassionate and understanding friend or mentor. How would they respond to the same situation or challenge you faced?

Rewrite the negative self-talk statements from Step 2, replacing them with compassionate, supportive, and understanding messages.

Example:

- "It's okay to make mistakes; everyone does. I can learn from this and keep growing."

3. Practice using this compassionate inner voice in your daily life:

- Whenever you notice negative or critical self-talk, pause and remind yourself that you have the power to choose a more compassionate response.

- Make a conscious effort to replace harsh self-judgment with understanding and self-kindness.

- As you continue to practice this approach, your compassionate inner voice will gradually become a more natural and automatic part of your internal dialogue

4. As you cultivate your compassionate inner voice, consider how it may influence your relationships with your internal parts:

5. How can a compassionate inner voice help you better understand, accept, and work with your Manager, Firefighter, and Exiled parts?

6. What impact might a compassionate inner voice have on your overall well-being, self-discovery, and personal growth?

- How can a compassionate inner voice help you better understand, accept, and work with your Manager, Firefighter, and Exiled parts?

- What impact might a compassionate inner voice have on your overall well-being, self-discovery, and personal growth?

7. Continue to practice self-compassion and self-kindness as you progress through the workbook, applying these principles not only to your True Self but also to your interactions with your internal parts.

CULTIVATING SELF-COMPASSION

SELF-COMPASSION MEDITATION

Objective: Practice a self-compassion meditation to cultivate kindness and understanding toward yourself and your internal parts, promoting emotional healing and well-being.

Instructions:

1. Find a quiet, comfortable space where you can sit or lie down without distractions. You may choose to sit in a chair, on a cushion, or on the floor, depending on your preference.

2. Close your eyes and take a few deep, slow breaths. Inhale deeply through your nose, filling your lungs completely, and then exhale slowly through your mouth. Allow your body to relax and release any tension or stress.

3. Bring your awareness to your heart centre, the area in the middle of your chest. Imagine a warm, loving light emanating from your heart, enveloping your entire body with kindness and compassion.

4. Silently repeat the following phrases to yourself, directing the loving energy from your heart toward your True Self:

- May I be safe.
- May I be healthy.
- May I be happy.
- May I be at ease.

5. Now, bring to mind one of your internal parts (Manager, Firefighter, or Exiled). Visualize this part and imagine directing the loving energy from your heart toward it, offering compassion and understanding.

6. Silently repeat the following phrases, directing them toward the chosen part:

- May you be safe.
- May you be healthy.
- May you be happy.
- May you be at ease.

7. Continue to practice this meditation, extending self-compassion to other parts within your internal system as you feel comfortable. You may choose to focus on one part per meditation session or include multiple parts in a single session.

8. When you are ready to conclude the meditation, take a few more deep, slow breaths. Gently open your eyes and return to your surroundings, carrying the feelings of compassion and understanding with you.

9. Practice this self-compassion meditation regularly to nurture a kind, supportive relationship with yourself and your internal parts. As you cultivate self-compassion, observe any changes in your emotional well-being, self-discovery, and personal growth.

COMMUNICATING WITH YOUR PARTS

INTERNAL DIALOGUE TECHNIQUES

Objective: Learn and practice various internal dialogue techniques to communicate effectively with your internal parts, fostering understanding, collaboration, and healing within your internal system.

Instructions:

1. Review the following internal dialogue techniques:

- Active Listening: Pay close attention to your part's thoughts and feelings, and demonstrate understanding by paraphrasing, validating, or empathizing with their experiences.

- Open-Ended Questions: Ask questions that encourage the part to explore and express their thoughts, feelings, or experiences more deeply, rather than seeking simple yes or no answers.

- Nonjudgmental Curiosity: Approach the dialogue with genuine curiosity, and avoid criticism or judgment. Show your willingness to learn and understand your part's perspective.

- Reflective Responses: Summarize or rephrase your part's statements to show you are actively listening and to clarify your understanding.

- Empathy and Validation: Acknowledge and validate your part's emotions, recognizing that their feelings are valid and important.

2. Choose a part (Manager, Firefighter, or Exiled) with which you would like to practice these techniques. In your journal, write a brief description of the part, its role in your internal system, and any current concerns or challenges it may be facing.

3. Begin a dialogue with the chosen part, using the internal dialogue techniques described above. Write down the conversation in your journal, focusing on active listening, open-ended questions, nonjudgmental curiosity, reflective responses, and empathy and validation.

Example:

True Self: I've noticed that you seem to be feeling overwhelmed and stressed lately, Procrastinator. Can you tell me more about what's been going on for you?
Procrastinator: I'm trying to protect you from feeling anxious, but there's just so much going on that it's hard to keep up.

True Self: It sounds like you're doing your best to help me manage anxiety in the face of many demands. What do you think would be helpful in this situation?

4. After completing the dialogue, reflect on the following questions in your journal:

- Which internal dialogue techniques did I find most effective or helpful in communicating with my part?

- What new insights or understanding did I gain about my part through this dialogue?

- How might practising these internal dialogue techniques support my personal growth, self-discovery, and healing process?

5. Continue to practice these internal dialogue techniques in your conversations with your internal parts, adjusting and adapting your approach as needed to foster effective communication, understanding, and collaboration.

COMMUNICATING WITH YOUR PARTS

CREATING A SAFE SPACE FOR YOUR PARTS

Objective: Develop a mental safe space where your internal parts can feel secure, valued, and heard, fostering communication, understanding, and healing within your internal system.

Instructions:

1. Find a quiet, comfortable space where you can sit or lie down without distractions. Close your eyes and take a few deep, slow breaths, allowing your body to relax and release any tension or stress.

2. Visualize a safe space where your internal parts can gather, communicate, and collaborate. This space can be a real or imagined place, such as a peaceful garden, a cosy room, or a serene beach. Consider the following questions as you create your safe space:

- What does this space look like?

- What sensory elements are present (e.g., sights, sounds, smells, textures)?

- How does this space make you and your parts feel?

COMMUNICATING WITH YOUR PARTS

3. Once you have a clear image of your safe space, invite your internal parts to join you there. Visualize each part entering the space and finding a comfortable spot to settle.

4. As your parts gather in the safe space, pay attention to their feelings and reactions. Take note of any parts that seem hesitant, resistant, or uneasy.

5. Direct your compassionate inner voice (developed in Exercise 12) toward these parts, offering reassurance and understanding. Encourage them to share their thoughts, feelings, or concerns within the safe space.

6. Spend some time in the safe space, allowing your parts to communicate and collaborate as needed. Observe their interactions and consider how the safe space can facilitate understanding, connection, and healing within your internal system.

7. When you are ready to conclude the visualization, take a few more deep, slow breaths. Gently open your eyes and return to your surroundings, carrying the feelings of safety and connection with you.

8. Continue to practice creating and visiting the safe space with your parts, using it as a tool for communication, understanding, and healing. As you develop a stronger connection with your parts and foster a sense of safety and trust, your internal system will become more balanced, harmonious, and resilient.

UNBURDENING YOUR PARTS

IDENTIFYING BURDENS

Objective: Recognize and understand the burdens that your internal parts carry, such as negative beliefs, unprocessed emotions, or unresolved trauma, to gain insight into their roles and functions within your internal system.

Instructions:

1. Review the concept of burdens in the IFS model:

Burdens are the negative beliefs, unprocessed emotions, or unresolved trauma that your parts carry. These burdens often stem from past experiences and shape the parts' roles and functions within your internal system.

2. Reflect on your own internal system and consider the following questions:

- Which parts of mine might be carrying burdens? Are there any that stand out as particularly significant or influential?

- What specific negative beliefs, unprocessed emotions, or unresolved trauma do these parts carry? How have they been impacted by past experiences?

3. In your journal, create a list of your parts that carry burdens. For each part, briefly describe the burdens it carries.

Example:

- The Abandoned Child (Exiled part): Holds feelings of loneliness and unworthiness stemming from childhood experiences of rejection or neglect.

4. Once you have identified the parts carrying burdens, take a moment to consider the following questions:

- How do these burdens influence my thoughts, feelings, and actions?

- Are there any situations in which the burdens carried by my parts are particularly active or noticeable?

5. As you progress through the workbook, use this list of parts carrying burdens as a reference for further exploration and self-discovery. You will have opportunities to deepen your understanding of these parts and learn strategies for working with them in a more compassionate and healing way, ultimately helping to unburden and release these burdens.

UNBURDENING YOUR PARTS

RELEASING BURDENS USING VISUALIZATION

Objective: Use visualization techniques to help your internal parts release burdens, fostering emotional healing, and personal growth.

Instructions:

1. Find a quiet, comfortable space where you can sit or lie down without distractions. Close your eyes and take a few deep, slow breaths, allowing your body to relax and release any tension or stress.

2. Recall the mental safe space you created in Exercise 16. Visualize this space and invite your internal parts to join you there.

3. Choose a part that is carrying a burden (identified in Exercise 15). Invite this part to share its burden with you in the safe space, creating an open, supportive environment for the part to express itself.

4. As the part shares its burden, visualize the burden taking on a physical form. This could be an object, a color, or even a symbol representing the burden.

5. Encourage the part to let go of the burden, releasing it from their grasp. As the burden is released, visualize it being transformed into a source of healing energy, such as a warm, glowing light.

UNBURDENING YOUR PARTS

6. Allow this healing energy to envelop the part, providing comfort, reassurance, and healing. Encourage the part to absorb the healing energy and integrate it into their essence.

7. Once the burden has been released and transformed, express gratitude to the part for their courage and trust. Acknowledge the part's willingness to let go of the burden and embrace healing.

8. Take a few more deep, slow breaths, and gently open your eyes, returning to your surroundings. Reflect on the visualization and consider any insights or emotions that emerged during the process.

9. Repeat this visualization exercise with other parts that carry burdens, working with one part at a time. As you help your parts release their burdens and embrace healing, observe any changes in your internal system, emotional well-being, and personal growth.

Remember, releasing burdens is an ongoing process, and it may take time for parts to feel comfortable letting go. Be patient and compassionate with yourself and your parts as you engage in this healing journey.

BUILDING TRUST WITH YOUR PARTS
───────────

ESTABLISHING A TRUSTING RELATIONSHIP WITH YOUR PARTS

Objective: Develop trusting relationships with your internal parts, fostering effective communication, collaboration, and healing within your internal system.

Instructions:

1. Reflect on your current relationships with your internal parts. Consider the following questions:

- Which parts do I feel most connected to or trusting of? Why?

- Which parts do I find it challenging to trust or connect with? Why?

In your journal, create two lists: one for the parts you feel connected to and trust, and another for the parts you find challenging to trust or connect with.

Choose one part from the list of challenging parts to focus on for this exercise. Write down the part's name and briefly describe its role in your internal system.

BUILDING TRUST WITH YOUR PARTS

- Active Listening: Pay close attention to the part's thoughts and feelings, demonstrating understanding and validating their experiences.

- Consistency: Show up for the part regularly, consistently engaging in dialogue and demonstrating genuine interest in their well-being.

- Compassion: Offer kindness, empathy, and understanding to the part, acknowledging their emotions and needs without judgment.

- Honesty: Be open and transparent with the part, sharing your thoughts, feelings, and intentions in a clear, honest manner.

- Collaboration: Work together with the part to find mutually beneficial solutions, addressing both their needs and the needs of the internal system.

2. Develop a plan to build trust with the chosen part, incorporating the strategies listed above. In your journal, outline specific steps or actions you will take to develop a trusting relationship with this part.

Example:

- Schedule regular check-ins with the part, creating space for open dialogue and active listening.

- Practice compassion and empathy during conversations, validating the part's emotions and experiences.

- Collaborate on developing healthy coping strategies to address the part's concerns while maintaining balance within the internal system.

BUILDING TRUST WITH YOUR PARTS

6. Implement the plan, taking time to reflect on and adjust your approach as needed. Observe any changes in your relationship with the part, as well as your overall well-being and personal growth.

7. Repeat this process with other parts on your challenging list, working to establish trusting relationships throughout your internal system. As you develop stronger connections with your parts, you will create a more harmonious, resilient, and balanced internal system.

BUILDING TRUST WITH YOUR PARTS

PRACTICING ACTIVE LISTENING WITH YOUR PARTS

Objective: Enhance communication with your internal parts by practising active listening skills, fostering understanding, trust, and collaboration within your internal system.

Instructions:
1. Review the concept of active listening:

Active listening involves fully concentrating on, understanding, responding to, and remembering what your internal parts are saying. It helps build trust, understanding, and collaboration within your internal system.

2. Reflect on your current listening habits with your internal parts. Consider the following questions:

- Do I genuinely listen to my parts, or am I just waiting for my turn to speak or respond?

- Do I validate and acknowledge the thoughts and feelings of my parts, or do I dismiss or minimize them?

- Am I attentive and present during conversations with my parts, or am I easily distracted by my thoughts or external factors?

BUILDING TRUST WITH YOUR PARTS

3. Choose a part (Manager, Firefighter, or Exiled) with which you would like to practice active listening. In your journal, write a brief description of the part, its role in your internal system, and any current concerns or challenges it may be facing.

4. Begin a dialogue with the chosen part, focusing on practising active listening. Write down the conversation in your journal, using the following active listening techniques:

- Give your full attention to the part, staying present and focused during the conversation.

- Avoid interrupting, allowing the part to express their thoughts and feelings without judgment.

- Paraphrase or summarize what the part has said to demonstrate your understanding and clarify any misunderstandings.

- Validate and empathize with the part's emotions, acknowledging their feelings as valid and important.

Example:

True Self: I've noticed that you seem to be feeling anxious lately, Protector. Can you tell me more about what's been going on for you?

Protector: I've been trying to protect you from possible rejection, but it's getting harder to keep up with all the social situations.

BUILDING TRUST WITH YOUR PARTS

True Self: It sounds like you're doing your best to help me avoid feeling rejected in social situations, and it's becoming overwhelming for you. Is that right?

5. After completing the dialogue, reflect on the following questions in your journal:

- How did practising active listening influence the conversation with my part?

- What new insights or understanding did I gain about my part through active listening?

- How might active listening skills improve my relationships with my internal parts and support my personal growth, self-discovery, and healing process?

6. Continue to practice active listening during your conversations with your internal parts, developing your skills and fostering effective communication, understanding, and collaboration within your internal system.

DEVELOPING HEALTHY BOUNDARIES

IDENTIFYING BOUNDARY ISSUES

Objective: Recognize and understand boundary issues within your internal system to promote healthier communication, self-care, and emotional well-being.

Instructions:

1. Reflect on your internal system and consider the following questions:

- Are there any parts that tend to dominate or control my thoughts, feelings, or actions?

- Are there any parts that feel ignored, dismissed, or neglected?

- Do I have difficulty balancing the needs and concerns of my various parts?

2. In your journal, create a list of parts that you believe may be experiencing boundary issues. For each part, briefly describe the nature of the boundary issue.

Example:

- The Perfectionist (Manager part): Tends to dominate my thoughts and actions, leading to excessive self-criticism and unrealistic expectations.

DEVELOPING HEALTHY BOUNDARIES

4. Choose one part from your list to focus on for this exercise. Write down the part's name, a brief description of its role in your internal system, and the nature of the boundary issue.

5. Consider the following strategies for addressing boundary issues with your parts:

- Communication: Engage in open, honest dialogue with the part, discussing the boundary issue and its impact on your well-being and internal system.

- Compromise: Work together with the part to find mutually beneficial solutions that address the part's concerns while maintaining balance within the internal system.

- Self-Care: Ensure that you are taking care of your own needs, both physically and emotionally, to promote healthier boundaries within your internal system.

- Assertiveness: Practice expressing your needs and boundaries clearly and confidently, without being aggressive or confrontational.

5. Develop a plan to address the boundary issue with the chosen part, incorporating the strategies listed above. In your journal, outline specific steps or actions you will take to resolve the boundary issue.

Example:

- Schedule a conversation with the Perfectionist part, discussing the impact of its dominance on my well-being and internal system.

DEVELOPING HEALTHY BOUNDARIES

- Collaborate with the Perfectionist to develop more realistic expectations and healthier self-talk.

- Practice self-care activities to promote emotional well-being and support healthier boundaries within my internal system.

6. Implement the plan, taking time to reflect on and adjust your approach as needed. Observe any changes in your relationship with the part, as well as your overall well-being and personal growth.

7. Repeat this process with other parts on your list, working to address boundary issues and promote healthier communication, self-care, and emotional well-being within your internal system. As you develop stronger boundaries and a more balanced internal system, you will experience increased resilience, self-awareness, and personal growth.

DEVELOPING HEALTHY BOUNDARIES

ESTABLISHING AND MAINTAINING BOUNDARIES

Objective: Learn to establish and maintain healthy boundaries with your internal parts, promoting balance, well-being, and effective communication within your internal system.

Instructions:

1. Reflect on your current boundaries with your internal parts. Consider the following questions:

- Do I have clear boundaries in place with my parts?

- Are my boundaries flexible enough to adapt to changing circumstances or needs?

- Do I effectively communicate and enforce my boundaries with my parts?

2. Choose a part from your internal system to focus on for this exercise. Write down the part's name, a brief description of its role in your internal system, and any current concerns or challenges it may be facing.

3. Identify one specific boundary that you would like to establish or strengthen with this part. In your journal, describe the boundary and its importance for your well-being and the functioning of your internal system.

DEVELOPING HEALTHY BOUNDARIES

Example:

- Boundary with the Worrier part: Limit the time spent worrying about future events to 15 minutes per day, to promote emotional well-being and reduce anxiety.

4. Develop a plan for establishing and maintaining the chosen boundary, using the following strategies:

- Communication: Clearly and confidently communicate the boundary to the part, explaining its importance for your well-being and the internal system.

- Consistency: Consistently enforce the boundary, gently reminding the part when it is crossed and redirecting the part's energy or focus.

- Flexibility: Remain open to adjusting the boundary as needed, responding to the changing needs and circumstances of your internal system.

- Collaboration: Work together with the part to find mutually beneficial solutions that respect the boundary while addressing the part's concerns.

5. In your journal, outline the specific steps or actions you will take to establish and maintain the boundary with the chosen part.

DEVELOPING HEALTHY BOUNDARIES

Example:

- Have a conversation with the Worrier part, explaining the importance of limiting excessive worrying for emotional well-being.

- Set a timer for 15 minutes each day to allow the Worrier part to express its concerns and worries.

- Practice mindfulness techniques to redirect the Worrier part's focus when the boundary is crossed.

6. Implement the plan, taking time to reflect on and adjust your approach as needed. Observe any changes in your relationship with the part, as well as your overall well-being and personal growth.

7. Repeat this process with other parts in your internal system, working to establish and maintain healthy boundaries that promote balance, well-being, and effective communication. As you develop stronger boundaries and a more harmonious internal system, you will experience increased resilience, self-awareness, and personal growth.

HEALING AND INTEGRATION

HEALING WOUNDED PARTS

Objective: Engage in the healing process for your wounded parts, promoting emotional growth, self-discovery, and resilience within your internal system.

1. Reflect on your internal system and identify a wounded part that you would like to focus on for this exercise. Write down the part's name, a brief description of its role in your internal system, and the nature of its wound or burden.

Example:

- The Abandoned Child (Exiled part): This part holds the pain of feeling abandoned and rejected during childhood, leading to feelings of unworthiness and fear of rejection.

2. Find a quiet, comfortable space where you can sit or lie down without distractions. Close your eyes and take a few deep, slow breaths, allowing your body to relax and release any tension or stress.

3. Visualize the wounded part in your mind's eye, inviting them to join you in a safe, supportive environment. Express your intention to help them heal and grow, creating an open, trusting atmosphere for the part to share their pain.

HEALING AND INTEGRATION

4. Engage in a compassionate dialogue with the wounded part, using the following techniques:

- Active Listening: Genuinely listen to the part's thoughts and feelings, demonstrating understanding and validating their experiences.
- Empathy: Offer kindness, understanding, and support to the part, acknowledging their emotions and needs without judgment.
- Reassurance: Provide reassurance and comfort to the part, reminding them of your presence, support, and commitment to their healing process.

5. Invite the wounded part to release their burden or wound through visualization, using a similar approach to Exercise 17. As the part releases their burden, visualize it being transformed into a source of healing energy, such as a warm, glowing light.

6. Encourage the part to integrate the healing energy, allowing it to soothe, comfort, and heal the wound. Express gratitude to the part for their courage and trust, acknowledging their willingness to let go of the burden and embrace healing.

7. Take a few more deep, slow breaths, and gently open your eyes, returning to your surroundings. Reflect on the healing experience and consider any insights or emotions that emerged during the process.

8. In your journal, document the healing process, noting the wounded part's experience, the visualization, the healing energy, and any insights or emotions that arose.

HEALING AND INTEGRATION

9. Repeat this healing process with other wounded parts in your internal system, promoting emotional growth, self-discovery, and resilience. As you engage in the healing journey, observe any changes in your relationships with your parts, your emotional well-being, and your personal growth.

Remember, healing is an ongoing process, and it may take time for your wounded parts to fully release their burdens and integrate the healing energy. Be patient and compassionate with yourself and your parts as you engage in this transformative journey.

HEALING AND INTEGRATION

CREATING AN INTEGRATED SYSTEM

Objective: Foster greater harmony and integration among your internal parts, promoting emotional well-being, personal growth, and resilience.

Instructions:

1. Reflect on your internal system and consider the following questions:

- How effectively do my parts communicate and collaborate with each other?

- Are there any parts that struggle to work together or find common ground?

- What steps can I take to promote greater harmony and integration among my parts?

2. In your journal, create a list of your internal parts, including Managers, Firefighters, and Exiled parts. For each part, briefly describe its role in your internal system and its current relationship with the other parts.

Example:

- The Caretaker (Manager part): Provides emotional support and nurturance to other parts, but may struggle to connect with the Critic.

HEALING AND INTEGRATION

3. Choose a pair of parts from your list that you would like to help develop a more integrated and harmonious relationship. Write down the names of the parts, their roles in your internal system, and a brief description of their current relationship.

4. Consider the following strategies for promoting integration and harmony among your parts:

- Communication: Encourage open, honest dialogue between the parts, providing a safe space for them to share their thoughts, feelings, and concerns.

-

- Understanding: Foster empathy and understanding between the parts, helping them to see each other's perspectives and appreciate their unique roles within the internal system.

- Collaboration: Facilitate collaboration between the parts, guiding them in finding mutually beneficial solutions that address their individual concerns and promote the well-being of the internal system.

- Flexibility: Encourage the parts to be open and adaptable, embracing change and growth within the internal system.

HEALING AND INTEGRATION

5. Develop a plan to promote greater integration and harmony between the chosen pair of parts, incorporating the strategies listed above. In your journal, outline specific steps or actions you will take to help the parts develop a more harmonious relationship.

Example:

- Schedule a conversation between the Caretaker and the Critic, allowing them to openly share their thoughts, feelings, and concerns.

- Encourage the Caretaker and Critic to practice empathy and understanding during their conversation, validating each other's experiences and emotions.

- Collaborate with the Caretaker and Critic to develop healthier communication patterns and strategies for working together more effectively.

6. Implement the plan, taking time to reflect on and adjust your approach as needed. Observe any changes in the relationship between the parts, as well as the overall functioning of your internal system.

7. Repeat this process with other pairs of parts within your internal system, working to create a more integrated, harmonious, and balanced environment. As you foster greater harmony and integration among your parts, you will experience increased emotional well-being, personal growth, and resilience.

CONFLICT RESOLUTION

IDENTIFYING INTERNAL CONFLICTS

Objective: Recognize and understand internal conflicts among your parts, promoting greater self-awareness, emotional well-being, and personal growth.

Instructions:

1. Reflect on your internal system and consider the following questions:

- Are there any parts that seem to be in conflict with each other?

- How do these conflicts impact my emotional well-being and overall functioning?

- What steps can I take to better understand and address these internal conflicts?

2. In your journal, create a list of pairs of parts that you believe may be experiencing internal conflicts. For each pair, briefly describe the nature of the conflict.

Example:

- The Planner (Manager part) and The Free Spirit (Exiled part): The Planner seeks to create structure and order, while The Free Spirit values spontaneity and freedom, leading to a conflict over how to approach daily activities.

CONFLICT RESOLUTION

3. Choose one pair of parts from your list to focus on for this exercise. Write down the names of the parts, their roles in your internal system, and a brief description of the conflict they're experiencing.

4. Reflect on the chosen conflict and consider the following questions:

- How does this conflict impact my emotional well-being, personal growth, and relationships?

- What are the underlying needs or concerns of each part involved in the conflict?

- How might greater understanding, communication, and collaboration help resolve this conflict?

6. Develop a plan to better understand and address the chosen conflict, using the following strategies:

- Communication: Encourage open, honest dialogue between the conflicting parts, providing a safe space for them to share their thoughts, feelings, and concerns.

- Understanding: Foster empathy and understanding between the parts, helping them to see each other's perspectives and appreciate their unique roles within the internal system.

- Collaboration: Facilitate collaboration between the parts, guiding them in finding mutually beneficial solutions that address their individual concerns and promote the well-being of the internal system.

CONFLICT RESOLUTION

6. In your journal, outline the specific steps or actions you will take to better understand and address the conflict between the chosen parts.

Example:

- Schedule a conversation between The Planner and The Free Spirit, allowing them to openly share their thoughts, feelings, and concerns.

- Encourage The Planner and The Free Spirit to practice empathy and understanding during their conversation, validating each other's experiences and emotions.

- Collaborate with The Planner and The Free Spirit to develop a balanced approach to daily activities that honours both structure and spontaneity.

7. Implement the plan, taking time to reflect on and adjust your approach as needed. Observe any changes in the relationship between the parts and the overall functioning of your internal system.

8. Repeat this process with other pairs of parts experiencing conflicts within your internal system, working to create a more harmonious, balanced environment. As you address internal conflicts and foster greater understanding, communication, and collaboration among your parts, you will experience increased emotional well-being, personal growth, and resilience.

NAVIGATING RELATIONSHIPS

UNDERSTANDING RELATIONSHIP PATTERNS

Instructions:

1. Reflect on your past and current relationships, including romantic, familial, and platonic connections. Consider the following questions:

- Are there any recurring patterns or themes in your relationships?

- How might your internal parts be influencing these patterns or themes?

2. In your journal, create a list of significant relationships in your life, both past and present. For each relationship, note any patterns, themes, or challenges you have experienced.

Example:

- Relationship with Alex: Difficulty with trust and emotional intimacy; the Protector part may be overactive, trying to prevent emotional vulnerability.

NAVIGATING RELATIONSHIPS

3. Choose one relationship from your list to focus on for this exercise. Write down the name of the person, the nature of your relationship, and any patterns, themes, or challenges you have experienced.

4. Reflect on the chosen relationship and consider the following questions:

- Which internal parts might be influencing the patterns, themes, or challenges in this relationship?

- How do these parts express themselves in the context of the relationship?

- What underlying needs or concerns might these parts be attempting to address?

5. In your journal, write down the names of the parts you believe may be influencing the patterns, themes, or challenges in the chosen relationship. For each part, describe its role in your internal system and its potential impact on the relationship.

Example:

- The Protector (Manager part): Seeks to shield me from emotional pain and vulnerability; may create barriers to trust and emotional intimacy with Alex.

NAVIGATING RELATIONSHIPS

6. Develop a plan to better understand and address the influence of these parts on your relationship, using the following strategies:

- Self-Awareness: Practice mindfulness and self-reflection to better recognize the ways in which your parts express themselves in your relationships.

- Communication: Share your insights and experiences with your partner or friend, fostering open and honest dialogue about your internal parts and their impact on the relationship.

- Collaboration: Work together with your partner or friend to develop healthier relationship patterns that honour the needs and concerns of both individuals, as well as your internal parts.

7. In your journal, outline the specific steps or actions you will take to better understand and address the influence of your parts on the chosen relationship.

Example:

- Practice mindfulness to become more aware of when The Protector is influencing my interactions with Alex.

- Share my insights with Alex and discuss ways to create a safe space for emotional vulnerability in our relationship.

NAVIGATING RELATIONSHIPS

8. Implement the plan, taking time to reflect on and adjust your approach as needed. Observe any changes in the relationship and the overall functioning of your internal system.

9. Repeat this process with other relationships in your life, working to create more harmonious, understanding, and integrated connections. As you gain insight into the influence of your parts on your relationships, you will experience increased emotional well-being, personal growth, and healthier interpersonal connections.

NAVIGATING RELATIONSHIPS

STRENGTHENING COMMUNICATION IN RELATIONSHIPS

Objective: Improve communication skills in your relationships by understanding the influence of your internal parts, fostering greater self-awareness, empathy, and understanding.

Instructions:

1. Reflect on your past and current relationships, considering the following questions:

- How effective is communication in your relationships?

- Are there any areas in which communication could be improved?

- How might your internal parts be influencing your communication style and patterns?

2. In your journal, create a list of significant relationships in your life, both past and present. For each relationship, note any communication challenges or areas for improvement.

NAVIGATING RELATIONSHIPS

Example:

- Relationship with Sam: Difficulty expressing emotions and needs; the People Pleaser part may be trying to avoid conflict or disapproval.

3. Choose one relationship from your list to focus on for this exercise. Write down the name of the person, the nature of your relationship, and any communication challenges or areas for improvement.

4. Reflect on the chosen relationship and consider the following questions:

- Which internal parts might be influencing your communication style and patterns in this relationship?

- How do these parts express themselves in the context of your communication?

- What underlying needs or concerns might these parts be attempting to address?

5. In your journal, write down the names of the parts you believe may be influencing your communication style and patterns in the chosen relationship. For each part, describe its role in your internal system and its potential impact on communication.

Example:

- The People Pleaser (Manager part): Seeks to maintain harmony and avoid conflict or disapproval; may make it difficult for me to express my true feelings and needs with Sam.

NAVIGATING RELATIONSHIPS

6. Develop a plan to improve communication in the chosen relationship, using the following strategies:

- Self-Awareness: Practice mindfulness and self-reflection to better recognize the ways in which your parts express themselves in your communication.

- Empathy: Develop empathy and understanding for both your partner's or friend's perspective and the roles and needs of your internal parts.

- Active Listening: Practice active listening techniques, such as paraphrasing and reflecting, to ensure that both you and your partner or friend feel heard and understood.

- Assertiveness: Cultivate assertiveness in expressing your thoughts, feelings, and needs, while respecting the thoughts, feelings, and needs of your partner or friend.

7. In your journal, outline the specific steps or actions you will take to improve communication in the chosen relationship.

Example:

- Practice mindfulness to become more aware of when The People Pleaser is influencing my communication with Sam.

- Share my insights with Sam and discuss ways to create a safe space for open and honest communication in our relationship.

- Work on active listening and assertiveness skills to enhance our communication.

NAVIGATING RELATIONSHIPS

8. Implement the plan, taking time to reflect on and adjust your approach as needed. Observe any changes in the relationship and your overall communication skills.

9. Repeat this process with other relationships in your life, working to create more effective, empathetic, and understanding communication. As you gain insight into the influence of your parts on your communication patterns, you will experience increased emotional well-being, personal growth, and healthier interpersonal connections.

MAINTAINING BALANCE AND HARMONY

MINDFULNESS TECHNIQUES FOR BALANCED LIVING

Objective: Learn and practice mindfulness techniques to promote balanced living, enhance self-awareness, and improve emotional well-being.

Instructions:

1. Choose a mindfulness technique from the list below to focus on for this exercise:

- Mindful Breathing: Focus on your breath as it naturally flows in and out, observing the sensation of each inhalation and exhalation.

- Body Scan: Mentally scan your body from head to toe, noticing any areas of tension or relaxation, without judgment.

- Loving-Kindness Meditation: Send loving-kindness and well-wishes to yourself and others, using phrases like "May I be happy, may I be healthy, may I be safe, may I be at ease."

- Mindful Eating: Savor each bite of food, paying attention to its taste, texture, and aroma, as well as the sensations of hunger and fullness.

- Mindful Walking: Walk slowly and intentionally, feeling the sensations in your feet as they touch the ground and observing your surroundings with curiosity and non-judgment.

MAINTAINING BALANCE AND HARMONY

2. Find a quiet, comfortable space where you can practice the chosen mindfulness technique without distractions.

3. Set a timer for 5-10 minutes (or longer, if you prefer) and begin practising the chosen technique, following the guidelines below:

- For Mindful Breathing, Body Scan (at the end of this module), and Loving-Kindness Meditation: Sit or lie down in a comfortable position, close your eyes, and focus on the sensations, thoughts, or phrases associated with the technique.

- For Mindful Eating: Choose a small snack or meal, sit down at a table, and eat slowly and intentionally, savouring each bite and paying attention to the sensations and experiences associated with eating.

- For Mindful Walking: Find a safe, quiet space to walk, such as a park or quiet neighbourhood, and walk slowly and intentionally, observing the sensations in your feet and your surroundings with curiosity and non-judgment.

4. As you practice the chosen mindfulness technique, your mind may wander or become distracted. This is normal. When you notice your mind wandering, gently bring your focus back to the technique without judgment or criticism.

5. After the timer goes off, take a few moments to reflect on the mindfulness practice and any insights, emotions, or sensations that arose during the exercise.

MAINTAINING BALANCE AND HARMONY

6. In a notebook or journal, document your experience with the chosen mindfulness technique, noting any challenges, insights, or emotions that emerged.

7. Practice the chosen mindfulness technique regularly, gradually increasing the duration of your practice as you become more comfortable and proficient. You may also choose to explore other mindfulness techniques to find the best fit for your needs and preferences.

8. Incorporate mindfulness into your daily life by finding opportunities to practice being present and non-judgmental in various situations, such as during conversations, household chores, or work tasks.

As you develop a regular mindfulness practice and incorporate mindfulness techniques into your daily life, you will experience increased self-awareness, emotional well-being, and a greater sense of balance and harmony in your life.

MINDFULNESS

MENTAL BODY SCAN

A mental body scan is a good, quick way to unwind and unpack the discomfort we are feeling. A mental body scan brings awareness to each individual part of our body finding the tension and discomfort and then relaxing that part of the body. The goal is not to completely rid yourself of all discomfort but to identify and manage it.

Get comfortable, preferably lying down. Take 5 deep breaths and start to relax. Bring awareness to your feet. Start with your toes, relax the muscles in your toes and continue to breathe slowly and deeply then move into the soles of your feet. If you feel any pain or tension acknowledge it and breathe through it. Move up to your lower legs and repeat the process. Continue to the upper legs, bum and pelvis. Repeat for the rest of the body. Record your pain/tension on the following page.

MINDFULNESS

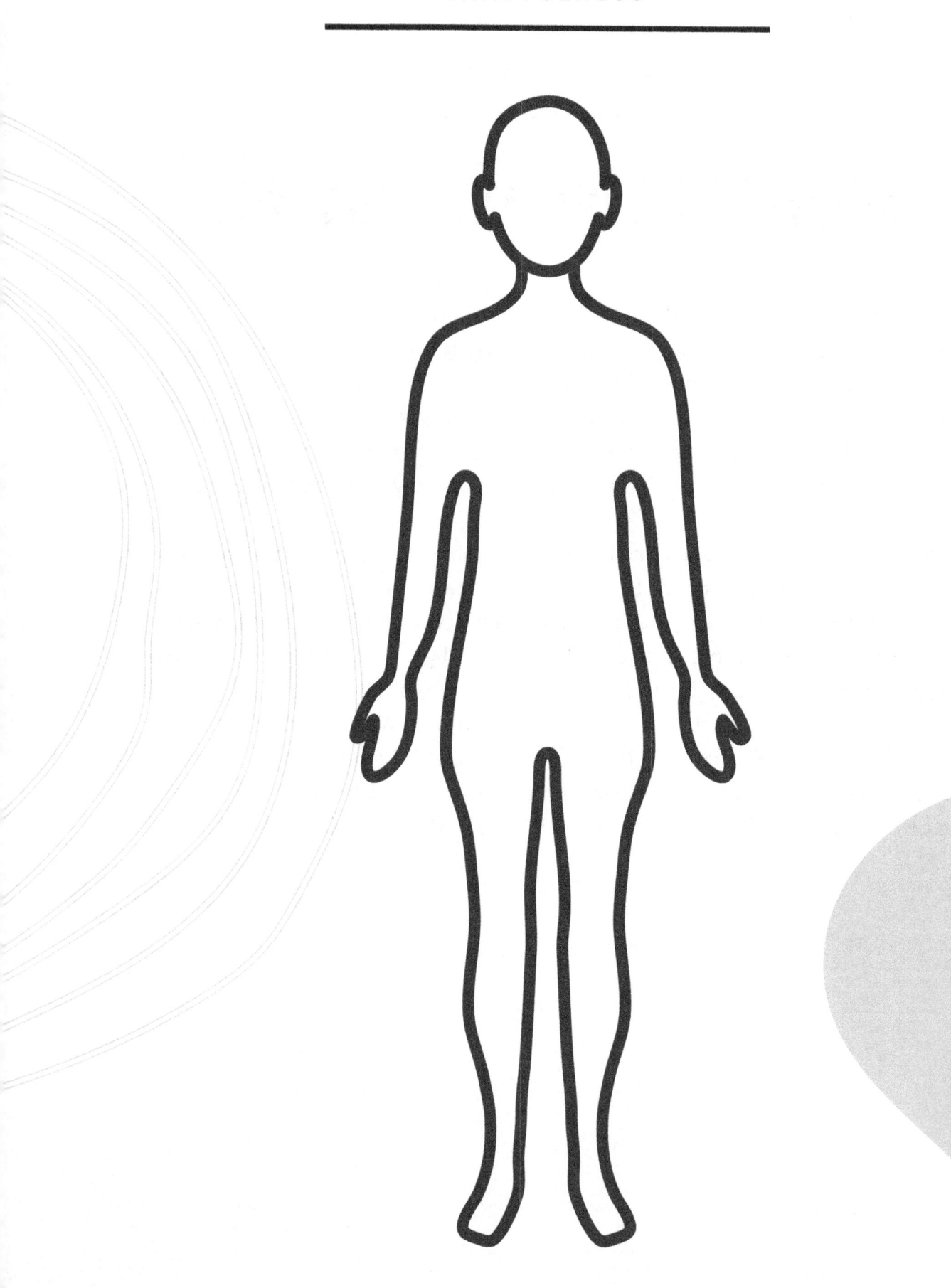

MAINTAINING BALANCE AND HARMONY

DAILY IFS CHECK-IN

Objective: Establish a daily practice of checking in with your internal parts to promote self-awareness, emotional well-being, and a harmonious internal system.

Instructions:

1. Set aside 10-15 minutes each day for your IFS check-in. Choose a consistent time and location, such as in the morning in a quiet corner of your home, to help establish this as a daily habit.

2. Find a comfortable position to sit or lie down, and take a few deep breaths to relax and center yourself.

3. Begin by inviting your True Self to be present during the check-in process. Remember that your True Self is characterized by qualities such as calmness, curiosity, compassion, and clarity.

4. Check in with each of your internal parts, one at a time. You may choose to focus on a specific part or explore various parts within your system. For each part, consider the following questions:

- How is this part feeling today?

- What is this part's role or purpose within my internal system?

- Are there any needs or concerns that this part would like to express or address?

MAINTAINING BALANCE AND HARMONY

5. As you check in with each part, practice active listening and empathy, ensuring that the part feels heard and understood. You may also wish to offer words of reassurance or support, depending on the part's needs or concerns.

6. After checking in with each part, take a moment to express gratitude to your internal system for their cooperation and participation in the daily check-in process.

7. In your notebook or journal, document the check-in process, noting the parts you focused on, their feelings, roles, needs, or concerns, and any insights or emotions that arose during the check-in.

8. Reflect on any patterns or themes that emerge from your daily check-ins, considering how these insights may inform your personal growth, emotional well-being, and interactions with others.

9. As you continue your daily IFS check-ins, you may choose to explore different parts of your internal system or focus on specific parts that require extra attention or care. The goal is to develop a deeper understanding and connection with your internal parts, promoting harmony, self-awareness, and emotional well-being.

By consistently engaging in daily IFS check-ins, you will create a stronger connection to your internal parts, foster greater self-awareness, and contribute to your overall emotional well-being and personal growth.

MOVING FORWARD

CREATING A PERSONALIZED IFS GROWTH PLAN

Objective: Develop a personalized IFS growth plan to support your ongoing personal development, emotional well-being, and a harmonious internal system.

Instructions:

1. Reflect on your experiences and insights from the previous IFS exercises, considering the following questions:

- Which exercises or techniques have been most beneficial for you?

- What areas of your life or internal system have shown improvement or growth?

- Are there any areas that still require attention or further exploration?

2. In your notebook or journal, create a list of personal goals related to your IFS journey. These goals may focus on improving self-awareness, enhancing relationships, developing communication skills, or addressing specific challenges within your internal system.

MOVING FORWARD

Example:

- Goal 1: Strengthen my connection to my True Self through daily mindfulness practice.

- Goal 2: Improve communication in my relationships by identifying and addressing the influence of my internal parts.

3. For each goal, develop a list of specific actions or strategies that will support your progress toward achieving the goal.

Example:

- Goal 1: Strengthen my connection to my True Self through daily mindfulness practice.

    - Action 1: Practice mindful breathing for 10 minutes each morning.

    - Action 2: Engage in a weekly loving-kindness meditation session.

4. Create a timeline for your IFS growth plan, specifying when you will begin working on each goal and any milestones or checkpoints along the way.

5. Review your IFS growth plan regularly, assessing your progress and making adjustments as needed. Celebrate your achievements and use any challenges or setbacks as opportunities for growth and learning.

MOVING FORWARD

5. Share your IFS growth plan with a trusted friend, family member, or therapist who can offer support, encouragement, and accountability as you work toward your goals.

6. Continue to explore and engage with IFS concepts, techniques, and exercises, incorporating new insights and strategies into your growth plan as appropriate.

By creating a personalized IFS growth plan, you will establish a clear roadmap for your ongoing personal development, emotional well-being, and harmonious internal system. This plan will provide structure, direction, and motivation as you continue to learn, grow, and evolve on your IFS journey.

CONCLUSION
───────────────

CONCLUSION: EMBRACING THE IFS JOURNEY

As you complete this IFS workbook and reflect on your experiences, it's important to recognize that the journey of personal growth and self-discovery is an ongoing process. Embracing the principles and practices of IFS can provide a powerful framework for understanding and nurturing your internal parts, fostering emotional well-being, and promoting personal development.

By engaging with the exercises and techniques outlined in this workbook, you have taken significant steps toward creating a harmonious internal system and strengthening your connection to your True Self. This process of self-exploration and growth can lead to increased self-awareness, healthier relationships, and a greater sense of balance and fulfilment in your life.

As you continue your IFS journey, remember to approach each new experience and challenge with curiosity, compassion, and openness. This mindset will support your ongoing growth and help you navigate the complexities of your internal system with grace and resilience.

CONCLUSION

CONCLUSION: EMBRACING THE IFS JOURNEY

Consider seeking additional resources, such as books, workshops, or therapy sessions, to further your understanding of IFS and its application in your life. Connecting with others who share your interest in IFS can provide valuable support, encouragement, and inspiration as you continue to learn and grow.

Finally, celebrate your progress and achievements along the way, recognizing that each step forward is a testament to your commitment to personal growth and emotional well-being. Embrace the IFS journey with an open heart and an open mind, and you will be well-equipped to navigate the complexities of your internal world and create a more harmonious, fulfilling life.

CONCLUSION

IF YOU FOUND THIS PACKAGE HELPFUL PLEASE TAKE 30SECS TO LEAVE A REVIEW

Thank you for choosing Therapy Courses. I hope that you found this workbook helpful. It took a long time to put it together and leaving a review helps a lot.

Thanks again,
Charlotte

IFS Journal

Can you think of any situations in your life where Manager, Firefighter, or Exile parts have emerged? Provide examples for each type of part.

How do you imagine your True Self? What qualities do you associate with it?

How do you imagine your True Self? What qualities do you associate with it?

How do you imagine your True Self? What qualities do you associate with it?

Are there any aspects of the IFS model that resonate with you or feel particularly relevant to your life?

Are there any aspects of the IFS model that resonate with you or feel particularly relevant to your life?

Are there any aspects of the IFS model that resonate with you or feel particularly relevant to your life?

Are there any aspects of the IFS model that resonate with you or feel particularly relevant to your life?

Which of these qualities resonate most with me when I am at my best?

Which of these qualities resonate most with me when I am at my best?

Which of these qualities resonate most with me when I am at my best?

Are there any specific moments or experiences in my life when I have felt connected to these qualities?

Are there any specific moments or experiences in my life when I have felt connected to these qualities?

Are there any specific moments or experiences in my life when I have felt connected to these qualities?

Are there any specific moments or experiences in my life when I have felt connected to these qualities?

_____
_____
_____
_____
_____
_____
_____
_____
_____
_____
_____
_____
_____
_____
_____
_____
_____
_____
_____
_____

How do I feel when I am connected to my True Self? What emotions or sensations arise?

How do I feel when I am connected to my True Self? What emotions or sensations arise?

How do I feel when I am connected to my True Self? What emotions or sensations arise?

How do I feel when I am connected to my True Self? What emotions or sensations arise?

TRUE SELF WORK

TRUE SELF WORK

TRUE SELF WORK

TRUE SELF WORK

TRUE SELF WORK

TRUE SELF WORK

TRUE SELF WORK

TRUE SELF WORK

Which practice(s) did I find most helpful in strengthening my connection with my True Self? Why

Which practice(s) did I find most helpful in strengthening my connection with my True Self? Why

Which practice(s) did I find most helpful in strengthening my connection with my True Self? Why

What changes, if any, have I noticed in my connection with my True Self? How has this affected my daily life or my work with my internal system?

What changes, if any, have I noticed in my connection with my True Self? How has this affected my daily life or my work with my internal system?

What changes, if any, have I noticed in my connection with my True Self? How has this affected my daily life or my work with my internal system?

What changes, if any, have I noticed in my connection with my True Self? How has this affected my daily life or my work with my internal system?

Which Manager parts do I recognize within myself? Are there any that stand out as particularly dominant or influential?

Which Manager parts do I recognize within myself? Are there any that stand out as particularly dominant or influential?

_____
_____
_____
_____
_____
_____
_____
_____
_____
_____
_____
_____
_____
_____
_____
_____
_____
_____

Which Manager parts do I recognize within myself? Are there any that stand out as particularly dominant or influential?

What specific roles or functions do these Manager parts serve in my life? How do they try to maintain control or protect me?

What specific roles or functions do these Manager parts serve in my life? How do they try to maintain control or protect me?

How do these Manager parts influence my thoughts, feelings, and actions?

How do these Manager parts influence my thoughts, feelings, and actions?

How do these Manager parts influence my thoughts, feelings, and actions?

What specific situations or circumstances activate this Manager part?

What specific situations or circumstances activate this Manager part?

What are the underlying motivations or fears driving this Manager part's actions? How does it aim to protect or support me?

What are the underlying motivations or fears driving this Manager part's actions? How does it aim to protect or support me?

LETTER TO YOUR MANAGER PARTS

LETTER TO YOUR MANAGER PARTS

LETTER TO YOUR MANAGER PARTS

LETTER TO YOUR MANAGER PARTS

LETTER TO YOUR MANAGER PARTS

What new insights or perspectives did I gain about this Manager part?

What new insights or perspectives did I gain about this Manager part?

Are there any patterns or beliefs that I need to address or reevaluate in relation to this Manager part?

Are there any patterns or beliefs that I need to address or reevaluate in relation to this Manager part?

Which Firefighter parts do I recognize within myself? Are there any that stand out as particularly dominant or influential?

Which Firefighter parts do I recognize within myself? Are there any that stand out as particularly dominant or influential?

What specific roles or functions do these Firefighter parts serve in my life? How do they try to protect me or cope with difficult emotions?

What specific roles or functions do these Firefighter parts serve in my life? How do they try to protect me or cope with difficult emotions?

___

How do these Firefighter parts influence my thoughts, feelings, and actions?

How do these Firefighter parts influence my thoughts, feelings, and actions?

Are there any situations in which my Firefighter parts are particularly active or noticeable?

Are there any situations in which my Firefighter parts are particularly active or noticeable?

What specific situations or circumstances activate this Firefighter part?

What specific situations or circumstances activate this Firefighter part?

What are the underlying motivations or fears driving this Firefighter part's actions? How does it aim to protect or support me?

What are the underlying motivations or fears driving this Firefighter part's actions? How does it aim to protect or support me?

Can I recall any specific experiences or memories when this Firefighter part played a significant role in my thoughts, feelings, or actions?

Can I recall any specific experiences or memories when this Firefighter part played a significant role in my thoughts, feelings, or actions?

CONVERSATION WITH YOUR FIREFIGHTERS

CONVERSATION WITH YOUR FIREFIGHTERS

CONVERSATION WITH YOUR FIREFIGHTERS

CONVERSATION WITH YOUR FIREFIGHTERS

CONVERSATION WITH YOUR FIREFIGHTERS

What new insights or perspectives did I gain about this Firefighter part?

What new insights or perspectives did I gain about this Firefighter part?

Are there any patterns or beliefs that I need to address or reevaluate in relation to this Firefighter part?

Are there any patterns or beliefs that I need to address or reevaluate in relation to this Firefighter part?

Which Exiled parts do I recognize within myself? Are there any that stand out as particularly significant or influential?

Which Exiled parts do I recognize within myself? Are there any that stand out as particularly significant or influential?

What specific emotions, memories, or beliefs do these Exiled parts hold? How have they been impacted by past experiences?

What specific emotions, memories, or beliefs do these Exiled parts hold? How have they been impacted by past experiences?

YOUR EXILED PARTS

YOUR EXILED PARTS

YOUR EXILED PARTS

YOUR EXILED PARTS

YOUR EXILED PARTS

What specific emotions, memories, or beliefs does this Exiled part hold? How have they been impacted by past experiences?

What specific emotions, memories, or beliefs does this Exiled part hold? How have they been impacted by past experiences?

Can I recall any specific experiences or memories that may have contributed to the formation of this Exiled part?

Can I recall any specific experiences or memories that may have contributed to the formation of this Exiled part?

CONVERSATION WITH YOUR EXILED PARTS

CONVERSATION WITH YOUR EXILED PARTS

CONVERSATION WITH YOUR EXILED PARTS

CONVERSATION WITH YOUR EXILED PARTS

CONVERSATION WITH YOUR EXILED PARTS

WEEKLY EXERCISES OF RECOGNIZING YOUR PARTS

WEEKLY EXERCISES OF RECOGNIZING YOUR PARTS

WEEKLY EXERCISES OF RECOGNIZING YOUR PARTS

WEEKLY EXERCISES OF RECOGNIZING YOUR PARTS

WEEKLY EXERCISES OF RECOGNIZING YOUR PARTS

What emotions did I experience today, and which parts were associated with those emotions?

What emotions did I experience today, and which parts were associated with those emotions?

Describe a situation where a part was activated or influential. How did it impact my thoughts, feelings, or actions? How did I respond to this part?

Describe a situation where a part was activated or influential. How did it impact my thoughts, feelings, or actions? How did I respond to this part? (See additional prompts + 100 prompt flashcards)

How do I speak to myself when I make a mistake, face a challenge, or experience a setback?

Are there specific parts (e.g., Manager or Firefighter) that tend to be critical, harsh, or judgmental in their inner dialogue?

_____
_____
_____
_____
_____
_____
_____
_____
_____
_____
_____
_____
_____
_____
_____
_____
_____

COMPASSION PRACTICE

COMPASSION PRACTICE

COMPASSION PRACTICE

COMPASSION PRACTICE

What new insights or understanding did I gain about my part through this dialogue?

What new insights or understanding did I gain about my part through this dialogue?

How might practising these internal dialogue techniques support my personal growth, self-discovery, and healing process?

How might practising these internal dialogue techniques support my personal growth, self-discovery, and healing process?

SAFE SPACE CREATION

SAFE SPACE CREATION

SAFE SPACE CREATION

SAFE SPACE CREATION

Which parts of mine might be carrying burdens? Are there any that stand out as particularly significant or influential?

Which parts of mine might be carrying burdens? Are there any that stand out as particularly significant or influential?

How do these burdens influence my thoughts, feelings, and actions?

Are there any situations in which the burdens carried by my parts are particularly active or noticeable?

RELEASING BURDENS

RELEASING BURDENS

RELEASING BURDENS

Which parts do I feel most connected to or trusting of? Why?

TRUST BUILDING

TRUST BUILDING

TRUST BUILDING

Are there any parts that tend to dominate or control my thoughts, feelings, or actions?

Are there any parts that feel ignored, dismissed, or neglected?

Do I have difficulty balancing the needs and concerns of my various parts?

Do I have clear boundaries in place with my parts?

Are my boundaries flexible enough to adapt to changing circumstances or needs?

___
___
___
___
___
___
___
___
___
___
___
___
___
___
___
___
___
___
___

Do I effectively communicate and enforce my boundaries with my parts?

How effectively do my parts communicate and collaborate with each other?

Are there any parts that struggle to work together or find common ground?

What steps can I take to promote greater harmony and integration among my parts?

Are there any parts that seem to be in conflict with each other?

How do these conflicts impact my emotional well-being and overall functioning?

_____
_____
_____
_____
_____
_____
_____
_____
_____
_____
_____
_____
_____
_____
_____
_____

What steps can I take to better understand and address these internal conflicts?

How does this conflict impact my emotional well-being, personal growth, and relationships?

What are the underlying needs or concerns of each part involved in the conflict?

How might greater understanding, communication, and collaboration help resolve this conflict?

Are there any recurring patterns or themes in your relationships?

How might your internal parts be influencing these patterns or themes?

Which internal parts might be influencing the patterns, themes, or challenges in this relationship?

How do these parts express themselves in the context of the relationship?

What underlying needs or concerns might these parts be attempting to address?

How effective is communication in your relationships?

How might your internal parts be influencing your communication style and patterns?

Which internal parts might be influencing your communication style and patterns in this relationship?

How do these parts express themselves in the context of your communication?

What underlying needs or concerns might these parts be attempting to address?

How is this part feeling today?

What is this part's role or purpose within my internal system?

Are there any needs or concerns that this part would like to express or address?

_____
_____
_____
_____
_____
_____
_____
_____
_____
_____
_____
_____
_____
_____
_____
_____

Which exercises or techniques have been most beneficial for you?

What areas of your life or internal system have shown improvement or growth?

Are there any areas that still require attention or further exploration?

Are there any areas that still require attention or further exploration?

Describe a time when you noticed a part of yourself reacting strongly to a situation. What was the situation, and what did the part want or need?	Think about a part of yourself that you are currently struggling with. What are its characteristics, and how does it influence your thoughts and behaviours?
Describe a time when you felt fully aligned with your Self. What did that feel like, and how did it differ from times when you felt disconnected from your Self?	Imagine meeting a part of yourself that you have never met before. What do you think this part would look like, and what might it want or need?

Write a letter from one of your parts to your Self. What does the part want you to know, and what does it need from you?	What are some of the beliefs that different parts of yourself hold about the world and your place in it? Are these beliefs helpful or hindering your growth and wellbeing?
Describe a time when you felt stuck or paralyzed by a part of yourself. What did that part want or need, and how did you respond?	What are some of the triggers that activate different parts of yourself? Are these triggers avoidable, or is it necessary to learn how to manage the parts that are activated?

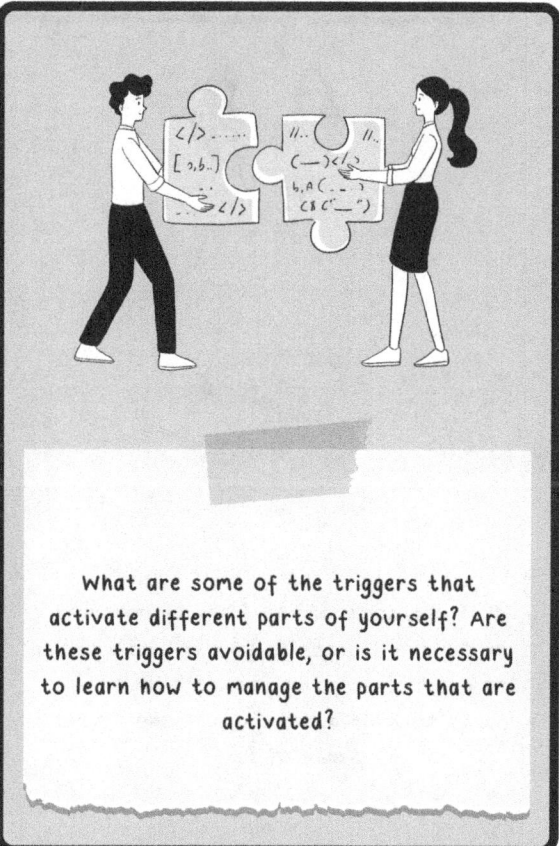

Write a list of your different parts, and describe their roles and functions in your life. Do you notice any patterns or themes among your parts?

Reflect on a recent conflict you had with someone else. What part of yourself was activated during the conflict, and how did it influence your behaviour and communication?

What are some of the fears or concerns that different parts of yourself hold about the future? How can you work with these parts to build a more secure and stable sense of Self?

What are some of the positive qualities or strengths of different parts of yourself? How can you tap into these qualities to support your growth and wellbeing?

Write a letter from your Self to a part of yourself that is currently struggling. What would your Self say to this part, and how would it offer support and guidance?	Describe a time when you felt like you were in a state of "flow" or "being in the zone." What parts of yourself were active during this time, and how did they work together to support your sense of Self?
Think about a part of yourself that you have been avoiding or denying. What might happen if you were to acknowledge and embrace this part?	How can I use my understanding of different parts of myself to deepen my relationships with others?

What are some parts of myself that I am curious to explore more deeply?	How do different parts of myself influence my creativity or sense of play?
What is a part of myself that I would like to release or let go of?	What parts of myself do I feel are most aligned with my values?

What are some ways that I can show appreciation to all parts of myself?

How do different parts of myself impact my sense of identity?

What parts of myself do I feel are most in need of healing?

How do I typically respond when a certain part of myself feels triggered?

What parts of myself do I feel are most misunderstood by others?	What is a part of myself that I would like to learn to love more deeply?
What parts of myself do I feel most disconnected from?	What are some things that different parts of myself are afraid of?

How do different parts of myself impact my self-care routine?	What parts of myself do I feel are supporting my growth?
What parts of myself do I feel are holding me back?	How do I typically feel when a certain part of myself takes over?

What are some common themes or issues that different parts of myself bring up?	How do different parts of myself influence my decision-making?
What part of myself am I most afraid to face and why?	What are some parts of myself that I am excited to explore or discover more about?

How do different parts of myself impact my ability to be present in the moment?	What parts of myself do I feel are most authentic or true to who I am?
What is a part of myself that I have been judging or criticizing too harshly?	How do different parts of myself impact my ability to set and achieve goals?

What parts of myself do I feel are most in need of self-care or nurturing?	What are some parts of myself that I feel are most creative or innovative?
How do different parts of myself impact my ability to trust or connect with others?	What parts of myself do I feel are most in need of boundaries or protection?

What is a part of myself that I have been neglecting or ignoring?

How do different parts of myself impact my sense of purpose or meaning in life?

What parts of myself do I feel are most resilient or able to bounce back from challenges?

What are some parts of myself that I feel are most in need of forgiveness or compassion?

How do different parts of myself impact my relationships with others?	What parts of myself do I feel most vulnerable or exposed when sharing with others?
What are some parts of myself that I feel conflicted about or have mixed feelings towards?	How do different parts of myself impact my sense of self-worth?

What parts of myself do I feel most proud of?	How do different parts of myself respond to stress or conflict?
What parts of myself feel most resistant to change?	What parts of myself do I feel are most reactive or impulsive? How do they influence my behaviour?

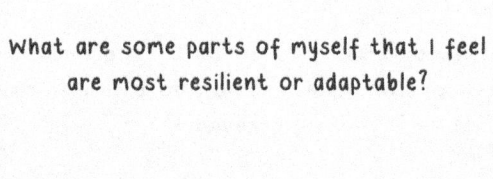

What parts of myself do I feel are most aligned with my goals and aspirations?	How do different parts of myself impact my ability to set boundaries with others?
What are some parts of myself that I feel are most resilient or adaptable?	What parts of myself do I feel are most aligned with my sense of identity?

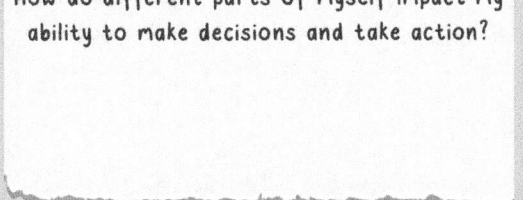

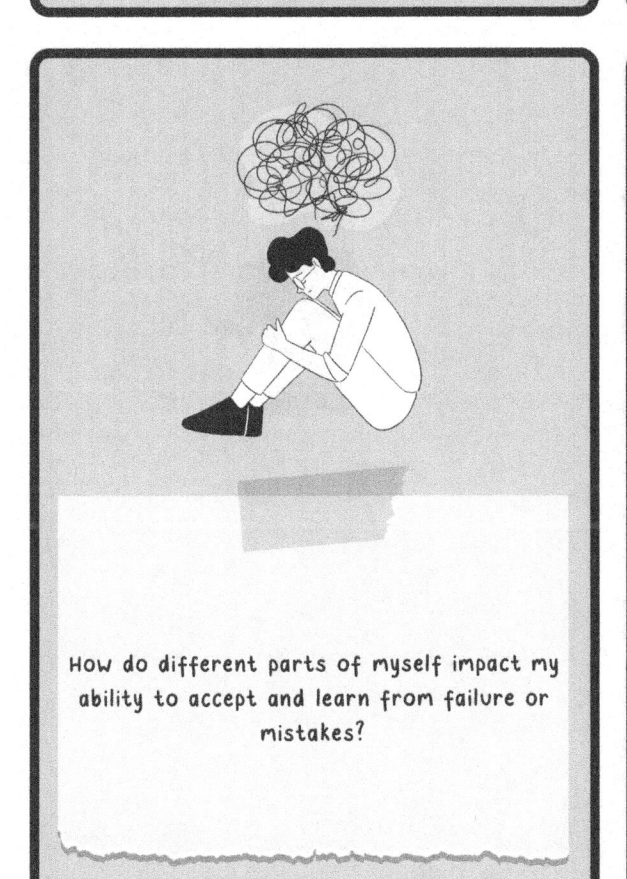

How do different parts of myself impact my ability to make decisions and take action?	What are some parts of myself that I feel are most in need of self-care or nurturing?
How do different parts of myself impact my ability to accept and learn from failure or mistakes?	What are some parts of myself that I feel are most in need of healing from past traumas or wounds?

What parts of myself do I feel are most aligned with my values around social justice or activism?	How do different parts of myself impact my ability to experience pleasure or enjoyment in life?
What are some parts of myself that I feel are most aligned with my sense of humour or playfulness?	What parts of myself do I feel are most protective or nurturing towards others?

How do different parts of myself impact my ability to be vulnerable or express my emotions?

What are some parts of myself that I feel are most aligned with my sense of intuition or inner wisdom?

What parts of myself do I feel are most disconnected or disengaged from my sense of community or belonging?

How do different parts of myself impact my ability to experience compassion or empathy towards others?

What are some parts of myself that I feel are most aligned with my sense of purpose or meaning?

What parts of myself do I feel are most in need of growth or development?

How do different parts of myself impact my ability to trust others or build healthy relationships?

What parts of myself do I feel are most resistant to change or growth, and how can I begin to understand and work with these parts more effectively?

How does my True Self differ from the roles and expectations I have taken on throughout my life?	What are some challenges I have faced in my life, and how have my internal parts contributed to my resilience and growth?
Which of my internal parts do I feel most connected to, and why?	What emotions or feelings do I find most difficult to express or accept, and how might this relate to my internal parts?

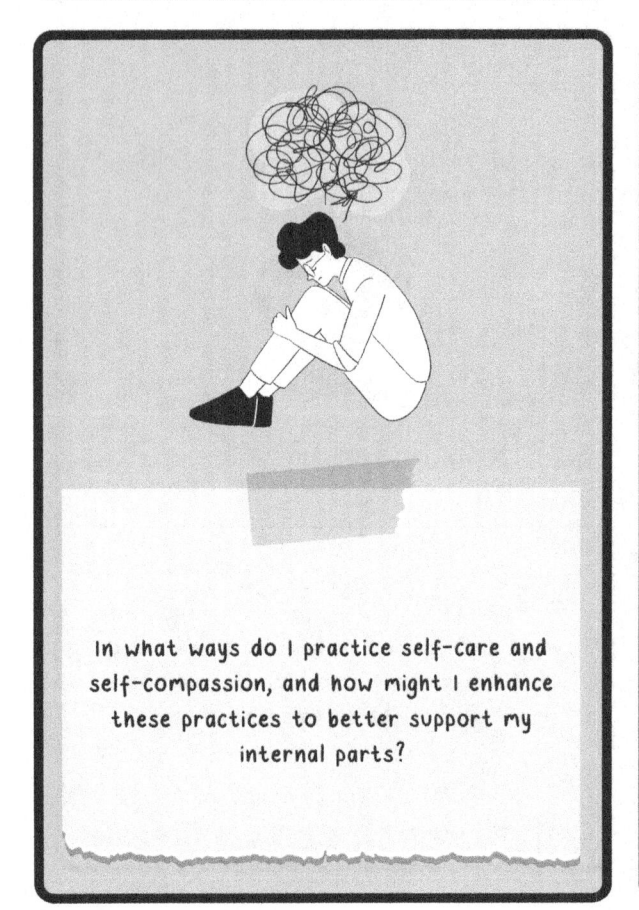

What are some of my core beliefs about myself and the world, and how might these beliefs be connected to my internal parts?	How have my relationships with others changed or evolved as a result of my IFS journey?
In what ways do I practice self-care and self-compassion, and how might I enhance these practices to better support my internal parts?	How has my understanding of my own emotions, thoughts, and behaviours changed through my exploration of IFS?

What are some of the key lessons or insights I have gained from my IFS journey so far?

How do my internal parts interact or communicate with one another, and what might this reveal about my internal system?

What are some of the strengths and qualities of my internal parts that I can appreciate and celebrate?

In what ways do my internal parts influence my decision-making and problem-solving abilities?

How can I create a more inclusive and supportive environment for my internal parts, both within my internal system and in my external life?	What are some of the fears or concerns that my internal parts may have about change, growth, or healing?
How has my IFS journey impacted my sense of identity and self-worth?	What are some of the goals or aspirations I have for my personal growth and development, and how can IFS principles and practices support these goals?

How do the various aspects of my life (such as work, family, and personal interests) align or conflict with the needs and desires of my internal parts?	How can I practice greater empathy and understanding for both myself and others, recognizing the complex interplay of internal parts that shape our thoughts, feelings, and behaviors?
In what ways do my internal parts support or hinder my ability to establish and maintain healthy boundaries in my relationships?	How can I continue to deepen my connection to my True Self and nurture a more harmonious internal system as I progress on my IFS journey?

How have my past experiences and relationships shaped the development and roles of my internal parts?	What are some strategies I can use to better manage conflicts or challenges that arise between my internal parts?
In what ways do my internal parts contribute to my creativity, passions, and interests, and how can I better support these aspects of my life?	How can I cultivate a stronger sense of trust and safety within my internal system, allowing each part to feel valued and supported?

Made in the USA
Coppell, TX
28 October 2023

23512120R00162